BASICS
OF THE
CHRISTIAN FAITH

MADE EASY

ROSE
PUBLISHING

Basics of the Christian Faith Made Easy
Copyright © 2022 Rose Publishing

Published by Rose Publishing
An imprint of Tyndale House Ministries
Carol Stream, Illinois
www.hendricksonrose.com

The *Made Easy* series is a collection of concise, pocket-sized books that summarize key biblical teachings and provide clear, user-friendly explanations to common questions about the Christian faith. Find more *Made Easy* books at www.hendricksonrose.com.

ISBN 978-1-62862-944-6

"14 Key Christian Beliefs" previously published as *Essential Doctrine Made Easy* © Norman L. Geisler

Scripture quotations marked NASB are taken from the (NASB®) New American Standard Bible,® copyright © 1960, 1971, 1977, 1995, 2020 by The Lockman Foundation. Used by permission. All rights reserved. www.lockman.org.

Unless otherwise indicated, all Scriptures are taken from the Holy Bible, New International Version,® NIV.® Copyright © 1973, 1978, 1984, 2011 by Biblica, Inc.® Used by permission of Zondervan. All rights reserved worldwide. www.zondervan. com. The "NIV" and "New International Version" are trademarks registered in the United States Patent and Trademark Office by Biblica, Inc.®

Scripture quotations marked NLT are taken from the *Holy Bible*, New Living Translation, copyright © 1996, 2004, 2015 by Tyndale House Foundation. Used by permission of Tyndale House Publishers, Carol Stream, Illinois 60188. All rights reserved.

Cover and page layout design by Cristalle Kishi

Photos and illustrations used under license from Shutterstock.com. Other photos by Soul devOcean/Unsplash, p. 4; Eugenio Hansen/Wikimedia, p. 18; Tim Green/Wikimedia, p. 22; stained glass: Alfred Handel, photo: Toby Hudson/Wikimedia, p. 30; Nheyob/Wikimedia, p. 91; falco/Pixaby, p. 93.

Printed in the United States of America
010422VP

CONTENTS

INTRODUCTION

THE world today holds an array of faith traditions, each presenting their own version of our relationship to God, what happens after death, and God's ultimate plans for the world. Perhaps you've been exploring the menu, familiarizing yourself with the tenets of different religions.

When it comes to the Christian faith, you may have found yourself asking questions like *What makes someone a Christian? What are their core beliefs? How do they believe an ancient book like the Bible can guide their faith and practices?* Or maybe you've wondered, *What are Christians really doing when they pray? Why pray to someone you can't see? What's the point behind customs like baptism and communion?*

It can be overwhelming trying to sort through the vast amount of information on these subjects. Whether you're on a personal quest to find God, someone who's simply interested in learning more about what Christians believe, or a seasoned Christian who needs help explaining your faith to a friend, *Basics of the Christian Faith Made Easy* aims to provide concise answers to these questions and more.

First, we'll take a look at the basis of Christian faith and how it's revealed in their collection of Scriptures, called *the Bible*, and from there we'll explore the Christian concept of God's character. Next, we'll zero in on the central historical figure of Christianity—Jesus Christ—and examine how Christians view his claims.

Once a person has placed their faith in Jesus Christ, or become a "believer," as Christians are sometimes called by their own, they seek to follow his teachings and emulate his character—a process called discipleship. We'll touch on what's involved and the practices and disciplines of discipleship, as well as baptism and the Lord's Supper, which have been part of the Christian church for centuries. Finally, we'll wrap up with what Christians believe about death, the afterlife, and God's ultimate plans for the earth and humanity.

If you would like to jump to a quick reference that summarizes key Christian beliefs, feel free to take a peek at the chapters at the back of this book—"Quick Reference: 14 Key Christian Beliefs" and "The Apostles' Creed." A short list of resources for further reading and study is also included at the very end.

If you want to dive in at the beginning, you'll learn some basics about the Bible—what it is and how Christians look to it as the authoritative source that describes who God is and how he relates to people. Are you ready to go? Let's get started!

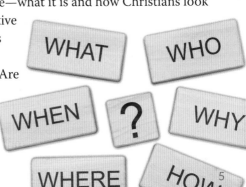

WHAT WHO WHEN ? WHY WHERE HOW

HOW DO CHRISTIANS KNOW ABOUT GOD?

God: It's a word that's thrown around a lot, but have you ever wondered who God is or whether God even exists? The Christian faith is one that holds a strong belief in a supreme being who is closely involved with the world he created. But what makes Christians so sure that there is a God, and from where do they draw their concept of who he is and what he is like?

In a nutshell, Christians point to (1) **the beauty and complexity of the world around us**, and (2) their collection of Scriptures, called **the Bible**.

Creation

Christians believe that the wonders of the world we see—and even the intricacies of the world we can't see—point to a supreme Creator. The universe with its myriad stars and galaxies ... the fact the earth is the perfect distance from the sun, making life sustainable ... the vibrant colors of a rainbow or a sunset ... our planet's thousands of unique (and often curious) plant and animal species ... the amazing craftsmanship of the human body ... Christ's followers claim that such beauty and majesty could only originate from a divine being. The following passages from the Bible illustrate this concept:

> *The heavens declare the glory of God; the skies proclaim the work of his hands. Day after day they pour forth speech; night after night they reveal knowledge.*
>
> PSALM 19:1–2

> *Ever since the world was created, people have seen the earth and sky. Through everything God made, they can clearly see his invisible qualities—his eternal power and divine nature.*
>
> ROMANS 1:20 NLT

The Bible

In addition to creation, Christians point to the Bible—a collection of ancient writings and letters—as the source that reveals God's identity, works, and character, as well as his plan for mankind. The Bible, Christians say, clearly shows that despite humanity's many failures, God still cares deeply for the people he created and is actively involved in their lives. But what exactly is the Bible, and what does it say? Let's take a closer look.

What Is the Bible?

Many think the Bible is a thousand-plus pages of religious restrictions and requirements, but Christians see this as a misconception. To understand their point of view, try looking at it like this: Imagine rooting around in your great-grandfather's basement. Buried in the corner next to an old phonograph is a big, overstuffed briefcase. Your heart races—maybe it's full of gold, jewels, or money!

Actually, it's even better than that. Within that leather portfolio you discover a treasure trove of old family documents: love letters and postcards, news clippings of major events, and tattered snapshots of relatives you didn't even know you had! You find birth and baptismal records, property deeds, marriage licenses, death certificates, and family genealogies. From that dusty satchel, you retrieve poems from someone's old journal, three or four outdated maps, plus a few vacation souvenirs. At the bottom of the briefcase, you even come across some old sheet music, a few "secret" family recipes, and folded-up building plans for your granddad's place, the old family homestead.

> The Bible is a written history of the people of God—an assortment of ancient texts by dozens of authors— kings, prophets, scribes, followers of Jesus, and others.

What you have stumbled upon, of course, is a family history. All those individual documents and artifacts combine to tell the unique story of a specific family—yours. In a real sense, this is what the Bible is. It's a written history of the people of God—an assortment of ancient texts by dozens of authors—kings, prophets, scribes, followers of Jesus, and others. These writings were composed over a period of some twelve to sixteen centuries! (For comparison's sake, Charles Dickens wrote *A Christmas Carol* in only six weeks.) After these biblical documents were written, they were copied, circulated, gathered together, guarded, recopied, and passed down through the generations.

Even though it's technically an anthology of sixty-six smaller books, the Bible tells one epic story. Like our "briefcase in the basement" example, the assorted books within the Bible include a variety of material. Among the first thirty-nine books of the Bible—what Christians call the Old Testament—are lengthy narratives of Israel's distant history and detailed records of moral and ceremonial law. Other Old Testament books consist of poetic or wisdom literature, and others are prophetic in nature.

The final twenty-seven books of the Bible—called the New Testament—include narratives of the life of Jesus and a history of the first three or more decades of the Christian movement.

These historical records are followed by a number of letters (some not much longer than a postcard) written to specific churches and individuals. The New Testament ends with the famous book of Revelation, an eye-popping book of wild imagery and heavenly visions of what is and what's to come.

Two Testaments, One Story

The word *testament* means "agreement" or "covenant." The Old Testament describes how the world began and the unfolding of good and evil. It testifies of God's sadness over humanity's sin and his promise to restore their relationship with him. This promise started to gain steam when God told an old man named Abraham that he would become a blessing to all nations and have a myriad of descendants and land that belonged to them. The books of the Old Testament

How Did We Get the Word *Bible*?

Our English word *Bible* comes from the Greek word *biblion*, which means "scroll" or "book." A similar term, *biblos*, was used to refer to the papyrus material shipped from the ancient port city of Byblos. Many biblical manuscripts were written on papyrus. The plural of *biblion* is *biblia*, and the term came to refer to a collection of holy writings or sacred scriptures. Jerome, a scholar in the fourth century who translated the Bible into Latin, called the books of the Bible "the Divine Library."

chronicle the ups and downs of Abraham's descendants, the Israelites, and God's faithfulness to his promises despite the unfaithfulness of his people.

The emphasis is on a deliverer—a Messiah, meaning "anointed person"—whom God will raise up to save his wayward people and all of humanity from the curse of sin and death. When the last book of the Old Testament was written, about four centuries before the time of Jesus Christ of Nazareth, God's people—the Jewish nation—and the rest of the human race were still groaning under the weight of sin.

> The Bible is a single story—the written record of God's efforts to seek and save humanity from the effects of a world broken by sin.

Christians see the New Testament as a record of how Jesus Christ of Nazareth revealed himself to be the Messiah— the great king and deliverer foretold by the prophets in the Old Testament—the fully human and fully divine Son of God. *Jesus* derives from his Hebrew name, Yeshua, and *Christ* derives from the Greek term *christos*, which means "anointed one." Christians see his life, death, and resurrection as God's way of inaugurating a new covenant between God and all humanity (both Jews and non-Jews). The New Testament also records the historical beginnings of this new covenant and the followers of Jesus, who came to be called Christians, as well as several letters and writings by leaders whom Jesus had appointed. As a whole, the writings of the New Testament help to establish and reinforce the basic beliefs and practices of the Christian faith.

The Bible, then, is a single story—the written record of God's efforts to seek and save humanity from the effects of a world broken by sin. It has one consistent, overriding message: We humans will remain restless until we stop running from God, turn to him in faith, and find rest in the love and forgiveness of Jesus Christ. Observant readers marvel at the many ways the Old Testament foreshadows the events of the New Testament, at how it ingeniously points to the coming of Jesus and completes the story of the Old Testament.

THE OLD TESTAMENT

To see how the text of the Bible came to be, we have to go back around 3,400 years. Here's the story in brief:

The Israelites, recently freed from Egyptian slavery, gathered at the base of Mount Sinai while Moses, their leader, went to the summit to meet with God. It was there that the Israelites entered into a covenant with God, and it was then that God revealed his will—his plans and promises for his people. The second book of the Bible, Exodus, describes the scene. It says that Moses "wrote down everything that the LORD had said" (Ex. 24:4).

A short time later, God gave Moses two tablets of stone said to be "inscribed by the finger of God" (Ex. 31:18). For Christians and Jews, this encounter is viewed as the beginning of the composition of the Torah, the first five books of the Bible—also known as the Pentateuch, the Law, or the five books of Moses.

For the next eight or so centuries, Israel wandered in the desert south of Canaan; settled in the promised land; lived under a series of judges and kings; constantly battled their enemies; gradually turned away from God; watched their nation disintegrate; went into exile; and then returned from captivity to rebuild their land.

During this long period, God inspired prophets, kings, scribes, and unknown individuals to write down stories, lessons, and principles that he wanted preserved for posterity. He had these writers chronicle historical events; compose poems, songs, and wise sayings; and also record chilling and thrilling prophecies. In time, all these writings became what Christians know as the Old Testament.

There are many details we don't know about the actual "creation" of the Old Testament: how in each instance this mysterious divine and human collaborative process worked; who specifically wrote each and every book; and when precisely each of these writings first appeared as ink on parchment.

But there is much we do know. We know that ancient Israelite culture was an oral culture. They carefully memorized, constantly repeated, and faithfully handed down the stories of God's marvelous acts in history. We know, too, that the ancient Israelites were literate; they could read and write. We know they kept written records. Given all these oral traditions and careful records, at any point, a person guided by the Spirit could have sat down and faithfully recorded whatever God wanted revealed. We also know that occasionally the prophets were explicitly commanded by God to put his messages in writing.

The writings of the Old Testament were copied and recopied many times over the centuries. Roughly from 500 BC to the time of Jesus in the first century AD was

How Did We Get the Word *Christian*?

The book of Acts in the New Testament says that believers in Jesus were first called "Christians" at a place called Antioch, located in modern-day Turkey. The name obviously stuck, but what does it mean? *Christ* comes from the Greek term for the Hebrew Messiah, *christos*, which means "anointed one." To be anointed in the Hebrew culture was to be set apart for some special service. It came to be associated in the Prophetic writings of the Old Testament with God's promised Savior from the line of King David—Jesus. The "-ian" ending indicates belonging or membership. Christian means "one who belongs to Christ," or "one who is a part of Christ."

an era when many scholars think the books of the Hebrew Bible were gathered and arranged into a widely accepted canon of Scripture. By the time of Jesus, the Hebrew Bible was frequently called "the Law, the Prophets, and the Writings," "the Law, the Prophets, and Psalms," or simply "the Law and the Prophets." The apostle Paul referred to the Hebrew Scriptures as "the old covenant."

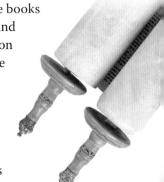

THE NEW TESTAMENT

Christians view the New Testament as a continuation and fulfillment of the teachings and prophecies established in the Old Testament. Here is a peek at what's in the twenty-seven books of the New Testament:

✦ **Four Gospels**
The New Testament begins with four accounts of the life and ministry of Jesus. (The word *gospel* means "good news.") The writers were Matthew and John (apostles of Jesus) and Mark and Luke (close associates of the apostles).

✦ **The Book of Acts**
Also called "Acts of the Apostles," this book is Luke's "sequel" to his gospel. In it, he chronicles the beginning and expansion of the early church in the first thirty or so years after Jesus. *Apostle* is a term

that comes from the New Testament Greek word *apostolos*, which means "one sent on a mission."

✦ **Twenty-One Epistles**
These letters were written to various churches and individual Christians.

✦ **The Book of Revelation**
This last book of the New Testament (and the Bible) is apocalyptic in nature, meaning that it envisions a great change in the world as God's kingdom is fully established on the earth.

WHAT IS GOD LIKE?

CHRISTIANS see the wonders and complexities of nature as signposts pointing to a creator God, and they see the Bible as the source that reveals who God is and what he has planned for the world and the people he made—a story that's still unfolding today.

History and modern-day culture are riddled with caricatures and ideas about God that don't necessarily square up with what the Bible reveals about his character. For example, there is the notion that God is distant and doesn't want to become involved with his own creation. Or that he is angry with sinful humanity, bent on punishing them with fire and brimstone should they make the slightest mistake. Or the opposite—that he is a God who will excuse anyone no matter what they've done.

It's important to understand how the Bible presents God's character since it provides the basis for Christian belief and practice. The overarching narrative portrays God as the one and only all-knowing, holy Creator, as well as a loving Father and faithful comforter and counselor. In response, Christians seek to draw near him through both individual and group practices, such as prayer and Bible study, and the biblical commands of baptism and communion.

So what exactly are the concepts of God's character that Christians draw from the Bible? Let's start with a summary of the basics.

One and Triune

A key Christian belief is that while being one, God—sometimes referred to as "the LORD" in the Bible—is triune as well, consisting of three distinct persons. It's easy to see that these two attributes exist in tension with each other. Christians agree that although both are correct, it's not easy to understand how they exist together.

✦ God is **one**. "Hear, O Israel: The LORD our God, the LORD is one" (Deut. 6:4). God is one in two ways: There is no other being like God, and God is the only real God. Because God is one, he is the only being worthy of praise.

✦ God is **triune**. God is one being who exists in three persons. God the Father, God the Son (Jesus Christ), and God the Holy Spirit are three separate persons, but they all share the same divine being and exist in loving relationship with one another. Christians call this unity of persons the "Godhead" or the "Trinity." Matthew 3:16–17 illustrates the concept: "As soon as Jesus was baptized, he went up out of the water. At that moment heaven was opened, and he saw the Spirit of God descending like a dove and alighting on him. And a voice from heaven said, 'This is my Son, whom I love; with him I am well pleased.'"

What Is The Trinity?

The Bible teaches that . . .

God is spirit. This means his essential nature is immaterial or nonphysical (John 4:24).

God is one. This means that there aren't multiple gods and that God's nature or essence is perfect unity (Deut. 6:4).

The one and only God exists as three distinct persons: God the Father, God the Son (Jesus Christ), and God the Holy Spirit. God is triune in nature. He is one, yet three. This is what people mean when they speak of *the Trinity*. For our finite minds, this "three-in-oneness" is an impossible-to-comprehend mystery, but the Bible reveals God as a Trinity of divine Persons existing in perfect unity (Matt. 3:16).

Each person in the Trinity is fully God—and yet not to be confused with the other persons of the Trinity.

+ The Father is God (1 Cor. 8:6).

+ The Son, Jesus Christ, is God (John 1:18).

+ The Holy Spirit is God (Matt. 28:19).

The following chart provides biblical support for the divinity of each person in the Trinity:

DIVINE ATTRIBUTES	FATHER	SON	HOLY SPIRIT
Eternal	✔ Rom. 16:26, 27	✔ Rev. 1:17	✔ Heb. 9:14
Creator of all things	✔ Ps. 100:3	✔ Col. 1:16	✔ Ps. 104:30
Omnipresent (in all places at once)	✔ Jer. 23:24	✔ Eph. 1:23	✔ Ps. 139:7
Omniscient (knows all things)	✔ 1 John 3:20	✔ John 21:17	✔ 1 Cor. 2:10
Wills and acts supernaturally	✔ Eph. 1:5	✔ Matt. 8:3	✔ 1 Cor. 12:11
Gives life	✔ Gen. 1:11-31	✔ John 1:4	✔ Rom. 8:10, 11
Strengthens believers	✔ Ps. 138:3	✔ Phil. 4:13	✔ Eph. 3:16

Transcendent and Infinite

God is *transcendent* and *infinite*. *Transcendent* means that he's beyond the universe and beyond human intelligence and imagination, meaning also that there are natural limits on how far our understanding of God can go. It also means that God is outside the universe and is only accessible because he reaches out to people first. God is also beyond understanding because he is *infinite*. This means that God is above our standards—he's not only wise and gracious; no one is wiser or more gracious than he is. It also means that God has no limits because he is beyond limits (1 Kings 8:27; Ps. 145:3).

Eternal and Creator

While being *infinite* refers to limits, being *eternal* refers to time. Christians point to Revelation 1:8 as one source that teaches God does not have a beginning or an end: "'I am the Alpha and the Omega,' says the Lord God, 'who is, and who was, and who is to come, the Almighty'" (see also Deut. 33:27; Jude 25). Before all things were, God already existed. Since God is eternal—he existed before anything else—it also means that he is *creator*. No one created God, but he created all things. God's existence doesn't depend on anything; he is free from obligation.

Omnipresent

As *eternal* and *infinite*, Christians also believe that God is not limited by space. God is *omnipresent*—present everywhere and in all moments of life. God is always accessible because he is always present. People can't hide from God or escape his rule over our lives. There is nowhere to run away from God; his love finds us everywhere: "As I was with Moses, so I will be with you; I will never leave you nor forsake you" (Josh. 1:5; see also Ps. 33:13).

Immutable

Since God is *eternal*, *infinite*, and *omnipresent*, Christians deem him as *immutable*—God doesn't change (Mal. 3:6; James 1:17). He will never become evil, or weak, or hateful, or cruel. God's attributes, essence, and nature will always be consistent and unchanged. His nature is reliable and trustworthy. These incommunicable attributes move Christians to worship God as awesome and glorious, pointing out that although he is so far away from any of our common experience, he still reaches out and desires to relate to us in personal, intimate ways.

Loving

The Bible actually defines God as "love": "Whoever does not love does not know God, because God is love" (1 John 4:8; see also Jer. 31:3). The Bible teaches that because of human rebellion and sin, God could justly destroy us—and yet because of his great love, God lavishes his grace and forgiveness upon those who ask: "In [Jesus Christ] we have redemption through his blood, the forgiveness of sins, in accordance with the riches of God's grace that he lavished on us" (Eph. 1:7–8). His love for people—and the love that exists among the persons of the Trinity—is an example to Christians of how to love. They believe that God's love is best seen in the sacrificial death of Jesus on the cross: "God demonstrates his own love for us in this: While we were sinners, Christ died for us" (Rom. 5:8).

Holy

While *love* drives God's grace, his *holiness* sets natural limits to how people can relate to him. Christians teach that it's not that God's love and holiness are in a struggle; rather, they complement each other. God is separated from sin and evil. Therefore, because people are sinful, they cannot approach God or even be near his holiness. But because God doled out his punishment for sin onto Jesus instead, those who realize their need for his forgiveness can enter into a relationship with God. Jesus' sacrificial death on the cross bridged the chasm between sinful people and a holy God (Lev. 19:2; 1 Peter 1:15).

Good

According to Christians, the engine that moves God's love to action is his *goodness*. People experience God's goodness in his love, patience, provision, and compassion. All good things in our lives come from God's goodness: "The LORD is good to all; he has compassion on all he has made" (Ps. 145:9; see also Rom. 2:4).

Just

Christians explain that as *holiness* balances *love*, God's *justice* balances his *goodness*. God is *just* because he judges with fairness and always does the right thing. God will judge the whole world (Rev. 20:13), and the wrongs will be righted: "The LORD ... does no wrong. Morning by morning he dispenses his justice, and every new day he does not fail" (Zeph. 3:5; see also Ps. 33:5).

Jealous

The Bible contains many examples showing that because of sin, the first inclination of many people is to reject God and offer their allegiance to lesser "gods" of this world: money, success, fame, career ... anything that brings them a sense of satisfaction and security—even good things such as family, friends, church activities, and country. This makes God *jealous* because by his nature, he cannot share his glory with anyone or anything. God wants first place in people's lives because he created them and loves them. He wants loyalty over any other thing: "Do not worship any other god, for the LORD, whose name is Jealous, is a jealous God" (Ex. 34:14; see also James 4:5).

Merciful

Although the Bible teaches that because of God's *justice*, "the wages of sin is death," God's *mercy* paves the way for "the gift of God [which] is eternal life in Christ Jesus" (Rom. 6:23). God is *merciful*. Out of his love and goodness, God mercifully withholds rightful judgment against sin and evil to allow the salvation of those who come to him in faith: "In your great mercy you did not put an end to them or abandon them, for you are a gracious and merciful God" (Neh. 9:31; see also Rom. 9:14–18).

Sovereign

God is *sovereign*. This means that he rules the universe and that he is not ruled by anything or anyone. Also, it means that nothing is beyond God's control: evil, death, blessings, hardships—all things happen within his authority. God has absolute *authority*, while humans have a limited authority in different areas of life. As a *sovereign God*, he provides faithfully for his creatures, in general, and for his people, in particular: "How great you are, Sovereign LORD! There is no one like you, and there is no God but you, as we have heard with our own ears" (2 Sam. 7:22; see also Dan. 4:32–35).

Faithful

An often touched-upon Christian teaching is that God is *faithful* to his word and will do just as he said, demonstrating goodness, mercy, and forgiveness to his people and releasing his justice in the world: "Praise be to the LORD, who has given rest to his people Israel just as he promised. Not one word has failed of all the good promises he gave through his servant Moses" (1 Kings 8:56; see also 1 Thess. 5:24).

Knowledgeable

God knows all things—he is *omniscient*, Christians say. God knows the past, the present, and the future, and he knows what's in every human heart. He knows what we think, say, and do. Nothing is a surprise to God. Nothing catches him off guard. Whereas God knows all things, human knowledge is limited by our condition as creatures. "Nothing in all creation is hidden from God's sight. Everything is uncovered and laid bare before the eyes of him to whom we must give account" (Heb. 4:13; see also 1 Sam. 2:3).

Omnipotent

Christians also believe that being the creator of all things gives God the authority to do whatever he pleases. He is *all-powerful—omnipotent*—but he never contradicts his nature. He can meet any need and help his people through any trial, no matter how overwhelming or impossible to overcome it may be. Unlike God who can do all things, humans have power limited by our condition as creatures. With the same power that raised Jesus from death, God will also resurrect Christians (2 Cor. 4:13–14; Isa. 40:25–26).

Patient

Christians affirm that God is *just* and *holy* and will judge all people; however, they emphasize that God is *patient* and slow to carry out his righteous judgment: "[God] passed in front of Moses, proclaiming, "The LORD, the LORD, the compassionate and gracious God, slow to anger, abounding in love and faithfulness'" (Ex. 34:6; see also 2 Peter 3:8–9). God waits patiently for people to turn from doing wrong and turn in faith to Jesus Christ, who appeased God's judgment and condemnation through his death on the cross.

Spirit

Finally, it is important to remember that according to the Bible, God is *spirit*. This means, first, that God does not have a body, while humans have both a spirit and a body. When the Bible speaks of God's face, hands, or body language, it is using comparison that we can understand and relate to. Since God is spirit, it also means that he is the source of all life. Because God is spirit, the Bible teaches that "his worshipers must worship in the Spirit and in truth" (John 4:24; see also Acts 17:24).

WHO IS JESUS CHRIST, AND WHAT DID HE TEACH?

THE Christian faith centers around the life, death, and resurrection of the historical figure Jesus Christ, who lived in the early first century. What we know about Jesus comes from the New Testament, as well as from a few sources authored by various Jewish and Roman historical figures. Christians believe that Jesus demonstrated through his teachings that he was the Son of God and Israel's promised Messiah. He announced that God's kingdom of love, mercy, and justice was coming to conquer the grip that evil had on the world. But how could he make such claims? Let's explore that question further.

Who Is Jesus? The Basics

God in the flesh (Luke 1:26–27). Jesus was born in ancient Israel to a virgin named Mary, a young Jewish woman. Jesus was conceived through the Holy Spirit, establishing his divinity in human form. Jesus was perfect and without sin or fault in all his thoughts and actions.

A teacher who had an earthly following (Matt. 4:23). When Jesus was thirty years old, he began to travel throughout ancient Galilee and Judah, teaching about the principles of God's kingdom and performing miracles of provision and healing. He gathered a core group of twelve followers, or disciples. Crowds of people were eager to hear his teachings and witness his miracles wherever he went.

> Jesus Christ's mission is to forgive sins, renew hearts, and offer abundant life and freedom that endures forever.

A friend of sinners (Matt. 11:19). Rather than despising sinful people, Jesus went out of his way to associate with irreligious people. They didn't avoid him; they flocked to him.

A great physician (Luke 5:31). During his brief ministry on earth, Jesus healed those who were physically, emotionally, and spiritually sick. His question to the world is still, "Do you want to get well?" (John 5:6).

A "good shepherd" (John 10:11, 14). Jesus proclaimed that he would protect people who don't have a clue what they're doing or where they're going. So many are vulnerable, just bumbling along and following the crowd, headed for danger. Jesus promised to protect them from predators and guide them to good places.

A crucified and resurrected Savior (Luke 19:10). The Bible claims that every human being needs to be rescued from something—

shame, guilt, fear, addiction, anger, unhealthy habits, toxic relationships, a life void of meaning. Jesus Christ came to willingly die a shameful death of crucifixion to take the punishment that sinful humans deserved. Because he is God, the grave could not contain him, and he rose to life three days later after enduring God's wrath for human sin. His mission then and now is to forgive sins, renew hearts, and offer abundant life and freedom that endures forever (Luke 4:18).

The supreme King (Rev. 19:16). The angel who announced the birth of Jesus introduced him as "a Savior ... the Messiah, the Lord" (Luke 2:11). Jesus is the one sent from God to rescue, restore, and rule everything. After being resurrected and appearing to his disciples for a brief period, Jesus ascended into heaven and "sat at the right hand of God" (Mark 16:19). There he awaits his assignment to return to earth, where he will no longer be a suffering servant but the reigning King over all.

The ultimate reflection of who God is (John 1:1, 14). The New Testament makes the claim that if people want to know what God is like, they need only look at the actions and character of Jesus as recorded in the Bible (John 14:9; Col. 1:15; Heb. 1:3).

What Did Jesus Teach?

Jesus came to proclaim that God's kingdom had arrived—
a kingdom that is "right now" but "not yet"—a kingdom
where God's light and love pierces the darkness that evil
and sin have brought to the earth he created. His kingdom,
foretold by Old Testament prophets, is "right now" because
Jesus came to forgive sins and renew hearts, and "not yet"
because he is still waiting to return to earth. At that time
he will rule as the supreme King and eventually defeat evil
once and for all. Jesus stated that only God the Father
knew when that time would be (Matt. 24:36). This present
time is set aside so that people will hear about Jesus Christ
and place their faith in his plan for salvation (Matt. 9:37;
Luke 10:2; Revelation 14:15).

Jesus sometimes used parables (short stories that illustrated
specific truths) to describe what the kingdom of God is
like and to teach his followers its principles. He also drew
on Old Testament imagery that his Jewish audience could
identify with since those were the Scriptures they knew
and followed. The idea of the kingdom uses an important
metaphor in the Old Testament: God is King (Ps. 47:7).
Kings in the ancient world had absolute power over their
dominions. However, they also had responsibilities toward
their subjects. Kings were supposed to:

✦ Provide protection for their territories and the people
  in them

✦ Provide for the needs of their subjects

◆ Maintain order in the kingdom, especially legal order

◆ Represent the culture's deity—in the Old Testament,
   Israel's king represented God's authority to the people

Like a king of the ancient world, Jesus Christ provided
these things for those who would pledge their loyalty to
him. He accomplished this by:

◆ Coming "to seek and to save the lost" (Luke 19:10) by
   "giv[ing] his life as a ransom" (Matt. 20:28), satisfying
   God's legal requirements for the penalty of sin

◆ Abolishing death (2 Tim. 1:10)

◆ Offering eternal life as a free gift to those who trust in
   him (John 3:16)

What Is "The Gospel"?

The word *gospel* is sometimes
used to describe the message
that Jesus taught, but what does
it mean? The term appears in the English New Testament and
derives from the Old English word *godspel*, which means "good
tale." So at its heart, *the gospel* means "good news" or "glad
tidings." The Bible presents the life, death, and resurrection of
Jesus as the ultimate good news because Jesus declared himself
to be the Messiah (John 4:25–26), the long-awaited Savior/King
God had promised to Israel in the Old Testament.

In one of his New Testament letters, the apostle Paul, a towering figure in the early church, summarized it this way:

> *I want to remind you of the gospel I preached to you, which you received and on which you have taken your stand ... that Christ died for our sins according to the Scriptures, that he was buried, that he was raised on the third day according to the Scriptures.*

> 1 CORINTHIANS 15:1, 3–4

In one short paragraph, this is the good news about Jesus Christ that Christians have been proclaiming for two thousand years. In just a few words it summarizes *the human condition*, *God's provision*, and *the decision* that people need to make in order to receive his provision.

The Human Condition

Notice Paul mentions Christ dying "for our *sins*." But what exactly does *sin* mean? People typically think of sin as the regrettable things we do or the awful things we say. But Jesus Christ taught that sin goes much deeper than that. Jesus says in Matthew 5:22–23, "You have heard that it was said to the people long ago, 'You shall not murder, and anyone who murders will be subject to judgment.' But I tell you that anyone who is angry with a brother or sister will be subject to judgment." External actions like lying, flying off the handle, looking at

The Bible describes the consequences of turning away from God as devastating and catastrophic.

pornography, being cruel toward others ... Christians assert that those are mere *outer* symptoms of a much deeper, *inner* problem.

In the divine story the Bible tells, we see earth's first couple, Adam and Eve, essentially declaring their independence from God (you can read about this in Genesis 3). That is sin in its essence: turning away from God, the source of life, and trying to find life and meaning apart from him.

The descendants of Adam and Eve—all of humanity—have inherited their same wayward nature (Rom. 5:12). Rebellion is in our spiritual DNA. In fact, the natural, default, 24/7 setting of every human heart is the tendency to tell God to take a hike when he tells us how to live. We resent his rules and rage against his commands.

The Bible describes the consequences of turning away from God as devastating and catastrophic. The apostle Paul states that the human race exists in a grim state of spiritual death (Rom. 6:23). People are "God's enemies" (Rom. 5:10), separated from the giver of life.

If you're thinking, *That doesn't sound like good news ...* you're right, of course! Fortunately, in the passage cited above, Paul explains what God did about this problem.

God's Provision

Paul declares that "Christ died for our sins ... he was buried ... he was raised." In other words, it is the death of Jesus Christ "for our sins" and his resurrection to life that opens the door for sinful humanity to experience the divine blessings of forgiveness and new, eternal life.

The good news that Paul and others announce is that when the human race was on death row because of sin, Jesus acted as our substitute by willingly taking the punishment we deserved (Rom. 5:8). Thus, Christ's death on the cross demonstrates two realities:

✦ God's justifiable wrath against sin (he hates whatever ruins his creation).

✦ God's remarkable love for sinners (he refuses to let us go).

By raising Jesus from the dead, God made it clear that his sacrifice for sin was acceptable. Now, as a risen Savior who has ascended into heaven where he intercedes for his followers, Jesus lives to offer forgiveness and eternal life to all who turn to him in faith.

The Faith Decision

The concept of *faith* forms the cornerstone of Christianity. At its essence, Christian faith is knowing about Jesus Christ, his teachings, and his voluntary sacrifice for the forgiveness of sins; embracing those concepts as truth; and engaging in an active decision of the will to live according to this truth. The apostle Paul's comments in 1 Corinthians 15:3 touch on this; notice how he directed his remarks to people who had "received" the good news of Jesus' death and resurrection: "I want to remind you of the gospel I preached to you, which you received and on which you have taken your stand."

> Salvation is a free gift from God; it isn't something that people can earn.

To receive the gospel is to embrace it. In the New Testament, *receive* is sometimes a synonym for *believe* (John 1:12)—to trust in Jesus Christ and the message of the gospel of salvation and take a stand on it. To receive it is to make it the foundation of one's life. Christians often express this sentiment in terms such as *repentance* (turning away from one's sins and toward God's path of forgiveness and right living), *receiving Christ* or *receiving forgiveness*, being *born again*, *having a personal relationship with God*, or *becoming a disciple of Jesus Christ*.

Christians also emphasize that the gospel isn't a marketing campaign to get people to come to church or a lecture about cleaning up their lives or a list of rules to follow so they can work their way back into God's favor. Rather, the gospel is the astounding announcement that through Jesus, God has come *to* sinful humanity and *for* their salvation: restoration in this life and eternal life in the renewed world that God will create. The New Testament is explicit: Salvation is a free gift from God; it isn't something that people can earn (John 4:10; Rom. 6:23; Eph. 2:8–9). There's nothing to do, because Jesus has already done everything necessary.

The Bible explains the good news of Jesus Christ in other passages, but 1 Corinthians 15:1, 3–4 is one of the most succinct. It shows the message and meaning of the gospel in one short paragraph.

Who Is the Devil?

The Bible reveals that God has an evil archenemy—the devil. He is also known as *Satan*, which comes from the original Hebrew word used in the Bible, meaning "adversary." Satan was originally a powerful, beautiful angel created by God. Satan became jealous of God's supreme power and rebelled, so God cast him out of heaven, along with the angels who had sided with him (Ezek. 28:11–17; Rev. 12:3–4, 7–9). For the sake of his own plans and glory, God has allowed Satan limited power, but ultimately he will destroy Satan in a lake of fire (Rev. 20:10).

The Only Way to God

Christians recognize that many people of other religions are good and moral people, but followers of Jesus stand by his own statements that only through him can people know God and escape the curse of sin and penalty of death. In addition, the Bible teaches that because the problem of sin is so deeply rooted in the human heart, it's only through Christ's gift of a new heart (becoming "born again," "born anew," or "reborn") that people can be saved; being a moral person or doing good deeds is not enough.

✦ **Jesus said he was the only way to God.** Jesus said, *"I am the way and the truth and the life. No one comes to the Father except through me"* (John 14:6).

✦ **Jesus said that he provides people with eternal life.** Jesus said, *"I give them eternal life, and they shall never perish; no one can snatch them out of my hand"* (John 10:28).

✦ **Jesus claimed to be God.** Jesus said, *"I and the Father are one"* (John 10:30).

✦ **Being a good, sincere person is not enough.** The Bible states, *"It is by grace you have been saved, through faith—and this not from yourselves, it is the gift of God—not by works, so that no one can boast"* (Eph. 2:8, 9).

✦ **People's hearts must be renewed.** Both the Old and New Testaments speak about a change of heart for those who trust in God's forgiveness through Jesus Christ: *"I will give them singleness of heart and put a new spirit within them. I will take away their stony, stubborn heart and give them a tender, responsive heart"* (Ezek. 11:19 NLT); *"Jesus replied, 'I tell you the truth, unless you are born again, you cannot see the Kingdom of God'"* (John 3:3 NLT); *"If anyone is in Christ, the new creation has come: The old has gone, the new is here!"* (2 Cor. 5:17).

The Three R's

Christians sometimes use "The Three R's" to describe what Jesus Christ has done for them.

First, he has **reconciled** them to God—united them again as sons and daughters of God by his death on the cross.

Second, he has **ransomed** them from being held hostage by sin, death, and the devil, or Satan—God's spiritual enemy who wants to destroy God's creation and the people he loves. A ransom is a price that is paid for release; to be ransomed is to be freed at a cost. Jesus' death was the ransom paid to free believers in Christ from that slavery to darkness and reconcile them to God.

Third, they are **redeemed**. To redeem someone or something means to buy it back again. Jesus' death paid the voucher, canceling the debt of sin owed.

The Journey of Discipleship

Once a person has placed their faith in Jesus Christ and trusts him for the forgiveness of their sins and the promise of eternal life, they nurture their new relationship with God through prayer, Bible study, fellowship with other Christians, and spiritual practices. This process of growth is sometimes referred to as *discipleship* and is facilitated through the work of the Holy Spirit. Discipleship helps a Christian to better know Jesus and his teachings; to grow more like him in character; and to serve him by loving others and making new disciples. Christians often view discipleship as a journey with high mountain peaks and occasional low valleys—a journey of which the final destination is eternal life with God in heaven. The Bible promises that along the way, Jesus will not leave his followers behind. We'll take a more in-depth look at discipleship in the next chapter.

Q. What is your only comfort in life and in death?

A. That I am not my own but belong—body and soul, in life and in death—to my faithful Savior, Jesus Christ.

THE HEIDELBERG CATECHISM, LORD'S DAY 1, Q&A 1

The Gospel Message: A Summary

1. God loves people, whom he created.

2. People are born with a sinful nature and bound to sin and cannot get free on their own.

3. God sent Jesus Christ to free them from sin and death.

4. Because of God's grace through Christ—not morality or good deeds—people can be assured of salvation and eternal life.

5. Becoming disciples of Jesus begins with repentance of sin and a request for forgiveness.

6. As disciples of Jesus, Christians grow and mature and deepen their relationship with God throughout their lives.

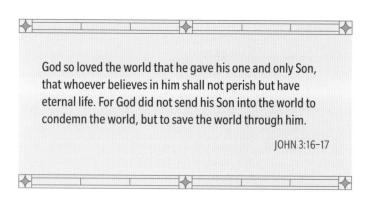

God so loved the world that he gave his one and only Son, that whoever believes in him shall not perish but have eternal life. For God did not send his Son into the world to condemn the world, but to save the world through him.

JOHN 3:16–17

WHAT IS DISCIPLESHIP?

CHRISTIANS sometimes refer to the process of growing in their faith as *discipleship*. The Greek word *disciple* means "student" or "learner." In New Testament times, a disciple entered into a master-apprentice relationship hoping to acquire wisdom and skills that could be imitated. The leader's expectation was that, once trained, the disciple would repeat the process. Jesus began his public ministry by urging people to "repent and believe in the gospel" (Mark 1:15 NASB). He then called those who were responsive to his message to become his devoted followers. According to Jesus, discipleship alters every facet of life: our beliefs, our essential nature, and our actions. Jesus' unlikely band of twelve disciples spent three years with him, listening to his teachings and observing his miracles. Christ invested huge amounts of time in his followers, training them and introducing them to a life of humble servanthood. As he modeled for them how to love (John 13:33–34), their lives were transformed by watching and imitating. After his death and his resurrection, and just before returning to heaven, Jesus called his followers together and commissioned them to help others learn to follow him.

> This is to my Father's glory, that you bear much fruit, showing yourselves to be my disciples.
>
> JESUS, JOHN 15:8

All authority in heaven and on earth has been given to me. Therefore go and make disciples of all nations, baptizing them in the name of the Father and of the Son and of the Holy Spirit, and teaching them to obey everything I have commanded you. And surely I am with you always, to the very end of the age.

MATTHEW 28:18–20

Discipleship today can happen in the context of a believer's own private study and practice and through study and fellowship with other Christians. And although discipleship underscores the importance of becoming like Jesus, the reality is that the process is often messy. Christians often fail in their attempts to follow Jesus' commands, disappointing and hurting others and themselves. Yet this is also an aspect that's normal and expected; even Jesus'

closest disciples experienced failure (Matt. 17:14–20; 26:36–40; Luke 22:54–62). The nature of discipleship requires that Christians learn to give grace to others and themselves as they persevere along the path of following their master.

One important key to understanding the motivation behind Christian discipleship, including its rewards and challenges, is to understand why *love* is the underpinning principle of the Christian faith.

Love: A Christian's Foundation

1 **The Bible states that the very essence of God's being is love.**

✦ "Love comes from God." (1 John 4:7)

✦ "God is love." (1 John 4:8)

2 **God's love defines how he interacts with the people he created.**

✦ "God so loved the world that he gave his one and only Son, that whoever believes in him shall not perish but have eternal life." (John 3:16)

✦ "This is real love—not that we loved God, but that he loved us and sent his Son as a sacrifice to take away our sins." (1 John 4:10 NLT)

45

3 **The Bible records that God gave the Ten Commandments as a basis for what it means to love God and others (Ex. 20:3–17):**

1 *"You shall have no other gods before me."*

2 *"You shall not make for yourself an image in the form of anything in heaven above or on the earth beneath or in the waters below. You shall not bow down to them or worship them."*

3 *"You shall not misuse the name of the Lord your God."*

4 *"Remember the Sabbath day by keeping it holy. On it you shall not do any work."*

5 *"Honor your father and your mother."*

6 *"You shall not murder."*

7 *"You shall not commit adultery."*

8 *"You shall not steal."*

9 *"You shall not give false testimony against your neighbor."*

10 *"You shall not covet … anything that belongs to your neighbor."*

4 *Jesus Christ told his followers that loving him meant obeying his commands.*

He also defined two of God's commandments as the greatest, stating they summarized all of God's commands and the messages communicated by his prophets.

✦ "If you love me, keep my commands." (John 14:15)

✦ "'Love the Lord your God with all your heart and with all your soul and with all your mind.' This is the first and greatest commandment. And the second is like it: 'Love your neighbor as yourself.' All the Law and the Prophets hang on these two commandments." (Matt. 22:37–40)

In essence, by loving God—treating him with reverence in their hearts and actions and demonstrating his loving and righteous character toward others—believers are doing what is most important to please God. For Christians, the basics of discipleship "made easy" boils down to what are called "The Two Greatest Commandments":

1. Love God with all your heart, soul, and mind (desires, actions, and thoughts).

2. Love others as you love yourself.

Self-Indulgence?

Jesus Christ's command that Christians love their neighbors as they love themselves might make some people pause because of the misconception that self-love is equated with selfishness and indulgence—character traits that go against the teachings of Jesus. But Christians look at self-love through a different lens. They realize that ...

◆ God is perfectly crafting them for purposes he has in mind. (Ps. 139:13–14; Eph. 2:10)

◆ God loves them with an intensity they can't understand and is turning everything in their lives into something that will bring good. (Rom. 8:28; Eph. 2:4–5; 1 John 3:1, 4:9)

◆ God entrusts them with gifts because of his love. (1 Cor. 4:1–2; 1 Thess. 2:4)

Christians emphasize that when they understand the value God himself bestows on them, they can love themselves in ways that reflect *his* love, providing the only foundation that will enable them to truly love others.

The Greatest Commandments

Jesus calls his followers to make love their greatest commandment because it's the commandment that helps them obey all his other commandments. It starts with loving God with the entirety of their being—heart, soul, mind, and strength. When Christians have that kind of love for God, they can express it as love for the world he sent them to reach. Love changes their character as they live out its principles, and it changes those who receive and experience a Christian's kindness. When practiced with increasing intensity by an ever-growing number of believers, Christians hope that demonstrating love will remake communities, cities, and entire societies. This is why Christian churches and organizations often have programs devoted to sharing the message of the gospel and humanitarian efforts such as food and clothing donations and crisis relief. Christians wholeheartedly embrace God's love for them and view discipleship as a way to obey his commands and express their love back to him in return.

> Discipleship is a lifelong process in which Christians will be far from perfect in living out Christ's teachings.

Discipleship Means That . . .

1 Christians learn to be imitators of Jesus (Eph. 5:1; 1 Thess. 1:6).

2 Christians seek to see people and the world as Jesus would—with love and compassion (2 Cor. 5:16).

3 Christians recognize that Jesus is King of their lives and the world (Phil. 2:9–11) and belong to him alone (1 Cor. 6:19–20; Rom. 14:8).

4 Christians grow in living out the "fruit of the Spirit" in their lives: "love, joy, peace, forbearance [patience], kindness, goodness, faithfulness, gentleness, and self-control (Gal. 5:22–23).

5 Christians become God's instruments, spokespeople, and envoys to testify of his goodness and love; to warn of the dangers of turning away from God; and to bring justice, act with love, and show mercy in a broken world.

It's important to note that because discipleship is a lifelong process in which Christians will be far from perfect in living out Christ's teachings, one of the main goals is to learn and grow from mistakes and support and encourage each other along the way.

Guiding Principles for Discipleship

1 **Knowing bad habits.** Christians often look for specific areas in their lives that need changing and ask God to give them the courage, strength, and help they need to face those areas.

2 **Confession.** Some traditions encourage confessing sins and shortcomings to a clergy member, and others emphasize that confessing directly to God is sufficient. However, the Bible does encourage confessing to another believer in order to receive prayer support and encouragement (James 5:16).

3 **Submission to God's call to change.** Christians point out that unless the effort to change is made by asking God for his help and grace, the effort will be in vain since Jesus said, "I am the vine; you are the branches. If you remain in me and I in you, you will bear much fruit; apart from me you can do nothing" (John 15:5).

4 **Accountability.** Having a trusted friend to report to, pray with, and be encouraged by is a key concept for successful Christian discipleship.

5 **Training.** This can include discipleship classes, Bible studies, outreaches, and the sheer discipline of substituting bad habits—sins—with good habits—virtue. Again, the emphasis is on relying on God's help for this through prayer and other Christian practices.

6 **Persistence.** Christians agree that discipleship is a lifelong pursuit that takes patience and persistence.

7 **Grace.** A hallmark of the Christian faith, grace applies just as much to a believer walking out their discipleship journey as it does to their initial experience of salvation. It is expected that Christians will experience failure, yet the point of grace is that the Holy Spirit is the one who renews and transforms. Instead of keeping track of every misstep, Christians are encouraged to focus on their growing relationship with God and be gracious with themselves and others.

> Grace applies just as much to a believer walking out their discipleship journey as it does to their initial experience of salvation.

8 **Gratefulness.** The Bible has much to say about maintaining a thankful attitude (Ps. 107:1; 1 Thess. 5:18). Christian discipleship is enhanced by thanking God for every small change that occurs and every victory after making a mistake, as well as thanking the people who help them along the journey.

"The Fruit of the Spirit"

One of the main goals of discipleship is for Christians to cultivate what is often referred to as *the fruit of the Spirit*. This phrase comes from a passage in the New Testament that instructs believers to let the Holy Spirit control their lives instead of sinful actions like rage, lust, bitterness, and envy. When they do, the "fruit" of the Holy Spirit's work in their lives will be evident:

> *The Holy Spirit produces this kind of fruit in our lives: love, joy, peace, patience, kindness, goodness, faithfulness, gentleness, and self-control. There is no law against these things! Those who belong to Christ Jesus have nailed the passions and desires of their sinful nature to his cross and crucified them there. Since we are living by the Spirit, let us follow the Spirit's leading in every part of our lives.*

GALATIANS 5:22–25 NLT

Through a combination of ongoing repentance, reconciling with those they have wronged, and the regenerating work of the Holy Spirit, Christians will grow to reflect these characteristics and live in the freedom they bring.

> Man's chief end is to glorify God, and to enjoy him forever.
>
> THE SHORTER CATECHISM OF THE WESTMINSTER ASSEMBLY

Knowing God, enjoying him, and becoming more like Jesus Christ are some of the extraordinary results of discipleship. We've just gone over some guiding principles, but stay tuned if you'd like a brief survey of the particular practices that help Christians enter more deeply into this mystery. We'll discuss these topics in the following chapter.

WHAT ARE CHRISTIAN PRACTICES?

God does not want his children to have a shallow, "Good morning—see you later" type of relationship with him but rather a deep, satisfying, loving, transforming relationship. Christian practices build the attitudes, emotions, thoughts, and actions that will promote this kind of relationship. However, it's important to note that Christians consider these practices a *result* of salvation and not a *means* of salvation.

Christian Practices Are …

+ Instruments of God's grace which, through the Holy Spirit, transform them daily into people who reflect Jesus' love, obedience, humility, and connection to God.

+ Activities that connect Christians in their common desire to obey God and follow his will.

+ Experiences that enrich their lives and the lives of those around them.

+ Activities that occur in the context of the church community; spiritual disciplines, although often practiced alone, are focused on building up fellow Christians as much as building up each believer.

+ Practices that bring hope despite failings and limitations: "He who began a good work in you will

carry it on to completion until the day of Christ Jesus"
(Phil. 1:6).

✦ Practices that permeate every area of a Christian's life
to train them for the life of faith, hope, and love they
believe Jesus has called them to.

Christian Practices Should Not Be ...

✦ Heavy loads of impossible, unrealistic, or unfair
expectations for people.

✦ Benchmarks to judge people's Christian maturity.

✦ Individualistic attempts to be holy or perfect.

✦ A measure of one's spiritual stature and strength.

✦ A way to hide sins with good works.

Common Christian Practices

Below is a list of common spiritual practices, by no means comprehensive, which many Christians have practiced throughout the centuries.

❶ *Prayer*

At its base, prayer is talking with God. Christians can pray alone or in a group; silently or aloud; using a written prayer, a prayer from the Bible, a liturgical prayer, or a spontaneous one. The Bible also portrays a life of continual prayer, meaning Christians live with an openness toward God in all they do (1 Thess. 5:17). The entirety of their lives can be a prayer, exhibiting praise and love to God.

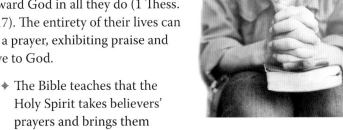

- ✦ The Bible teaches that the Holy Spirit takes believers' prayers and brings them before God the Father, while also interpreting the thoughts and desires of a believer's heart when they aren't sure what to pray or how to pray (Rom. 8:26–27).

- ✦ Christians have a transformational view of prayer: Prayer doesn't change God's mind about something; instead, the Holy Spirit uses a believer's prayers to shed light on who they are, what they need, and how they can please God.

WHY DO CHRISTIANS PRAY?

Prayer Draws Christians Closer to God. The Bible instructs believers to make prayer a high priority because God wants to partner with his people. Prayer is a way to demonstrate humility, dependence on God, and compassion for others (Col. 4:2; 1 Tim. 2:1). In prayer, Christians worship God, confess their sins, bring their requests, and wait and listen for God to speak. In short, Christians enter deeply and directly into relationship with God. Through communion with him, Christians believe (1) their hearts and minds will be changed to be more like Jesus Christ, and (2) they will grow to know his will for their lives (Rom. 12:2; 2 Cor. 3:18).

Prayer Brings Change. God not only hears a believers' prayers but also acts on them, bringing about real change in particular situations, in the world, and in the lives of the people they pray for (Matt. 7: 7–8; 21:22;1 John 3:21–22).

Prayer Brings Peace. The Bible instructs Christians to turn their anxieties over to God, who will give them peace of mind (Phil. 4:6–7).

Prayer Brings Protection. Jesus showed his followers the importance of praying for protection:

- ✦ **Jesus' prayer for his disciples:** "My prayer is not that you take them out of the world but that you protect them from the evil one." (John 17:15)

- ✦ **The Lord's Prayer:** "Lead us not into temptation, but deliver us from the evil one." (Matt. 6:13)

✦ **Jesus warned his disciples:** "Be always on the watch, and pray that you may be able to escape all that is about to happen, and that you may be able to stand before the Son of Man [Jesus Christ]." (Luke 21:36)

✦ **Also see** 2 Cor. 10:4 and Eph. 6:10–18.

❷ *Worship and Fellowship*

Worship is more than simply singing, praying, and attending church services. At its core, worship is an attitude of awe and gratitude, of humble submission to God's greatness and grace, of obedience and love. Christians see every activity and every relationship in daily life as an opportunity to worship God, so in this sense, Christians can worship alone. However, Christians think of the church as a family where people care about, support, teach, and encourage one another, so they also place high importance on worshiping corporately, as the Bible instructs (Heb. 10:24–25). Churches usually hold a weekly worship service led by a priest or pastor, with the format of the service varying. Many churches have regular programs such as Bible classes, youth groups, outreaches, and service projects.

> Sweet hour of prayer! Sweet hour of prayer!
>
> That calls me from a world of care,
>
> And bids me at my Father's throne
>
> Make all my wants and wishes known.
>
> WILLIAM WALFORD, STANZA 1 FROM THE CHRISTIAN HYMN "SWEET HOUR OF PRAYER"

WHAT DOES THE WORD *CHURCH* MEAN?

Church is a term that can have different meanings depending on the context. Most people are familiar with this word in connection with a church building or in connection with a particular building or a group of believers. The Bible, however, uses it in a more organic way to describe the entire community of Christians—not in relation to a physical building but to represent their identity as followers of Jesus Christ.

✦ The word can refer to a group of Christians located in a certain geographic area at a specific point in time.

✦ It can be a way of identifying people of biblical faith throughout all generations.

✦ The church is sometimes referred to as "the body of Christ"—a phrase used several times in the New Testament to indicate that individual believers have different gifts and talents that, when joined in unity with those of other believers, reflect the heart and character of Jesus Christ (Rom. 12:4–5; 1 Cor. 12:12, 27; Eph. 4:4; Col. 1:18, 24).

✦ The Bible also describes the church as a "spiritual" building where each believer fits like a custom-cut stone (1 Peter 2:4, 5) that is part of an earthly temple housing God's Spirit (1 Cor. 3:16–17; 2 Cor. 6:16; Eph. 2:19–22).

3 *Bible Study*

Reading and studying the Bible—also called "the Scriptures"—is a vital way to stay connected to God.

+ Scripture reading is the lifeblood of the church. The Bible equips, trains, and empowers Christians to fulfill God's calling (2 Tim. 3:17; 2 Peter 1:3–11; Heb. 13:21).

+ Scripture reading and studying can involve different activities: memorization, reflection, and transformative study using resources such as individual or group Bible studies and discipleship programs; study Bibles with notes and cross-references; commentaries; Greek and Hebrew lexicons; and Bible dictionaries, concordances, maps, and encyclopedias.

Christian Identity and the Bible

When Christians read the Bible, they learn more about who they are as God's people, where they came from, why they are here, and where they are going. The stories of the Patriarchs of the faith, as well as the books that record Israel's history, show how God relates to imperfect people who trust in him. The book of Psalms offers Christians a vocabulary to praise God, to express grief, and to pray for help. In the books of the Prophets, Christians learn what it means to be God's people in moments of difficulties and challenges and what it means to fail and receive God's grace and forgiveness. In the stories of the early church, Christians observe how the Holy Spirit guides and trains his church to carry on God's mission. When Christians read the Bible, their identity merges with that of the history of God's people. In this process, they mature in their faith and learn to teach others how to become part of God's story of salvation.

4 Service

The emphasis Christians place on service is rooted in Jesus Christ's teaching that true greatness is found in serving others (Matt. 20: 26–27; Mark 9:35). Jesus himself illustrated the importance of service when he washed his disciples' feet (Mark 10:43–45; John 13:4–17). Christian service begins by caring for one's own family (1 Tim. 5:8) and branches out to helping widows, orphans, and the poor

(Ex. 22:21–24; Ps. 82:3; Zech. 7:9–10; James 1:27; 2:14–17). By serving others, Christians become channels of God's love and compassion.

5 *Evangelism*

In the original Greek copies of the New Testament, the word used for *gospel* is *euangelion*. Thus in our English translations, one who proclaims the gospel is called an evangelist (2 Tim. 4:5). And when evangelists declare the story of Jesus' life, death, and resurrection, they are said to be *evangelizing* or doing *evangelism* (Acts 14:7). There are many tools and programs that help Christians obey Jesus' command to evangelize (Matt. 28:16–20), but many believers agree that the best way to evangelize is by developing close relationships with the people around them and demonstrating Christ's love in practical ways.

6 *Financial Giving*

Many Christians emphasize the importance of giving financial resources to support the work of the church and those in need, for at least three reasons: (1) Giving demonstrates their devotion to Jesus Christ and signifies that he is their number one priority (Matt. 6:24); (2) Christians believe that all they own belongs to God (Ps. 24:1); and (3) The Bible includes several passages where sacrificial giving is taught, encouraged, or demonstrated.

7 *Fasting*

For Christians, fasting is a period of time to abstain from something central to daily life as a reminder of God's sustaining power and their humble position before him. They often combine fasting with periods of devoted prayer and time in the Scriptures. In the Bible, each example of fasting includes a person or a group giving up food—and sometimes water too—either completely or partially. However, people today can fast in a variety of ways. For example, since screens have become such a significant part of everyday existence, turning off phones, TVs, and computers has become another means of fasting.

WHY DO CHRISTIANS FAST?

- ✦ To worship God and facilitate a deeper sense of intimacy with him (Luke 12:29–31; John 6:27, 33–35)

- ✦ To reveal their weaknesses, forcing them to rely on God instead of their own strength (Deut. 8:3; Matt 4:4)

- ✦ To ask God to move powerfully in their lives and in the world (1 Sam. 7:6; Neh. 1:3–11; Acts 13:2–3; 14:23)

8 *Solitude*

Christians are aware that the distractions of a busy world can hinder them from hearing God's voice and discerning his signals. Just as bodies need physical rest, minds, hearts, and souls need intellectual, emotional, and spiritual rest. Solitude is sometimes practiced by setting aside an hour, a day, a week, or any period of time to focus on God.

9 *Discernment*

Discernment is the Holy Spirit–inspired ability to separate a Christian's imperfect will from God's perfect will in recognizing, judging, and choosing what is right, good, and pure from what is wrong, evil, and impure. All Christians are called to be wise and discerning (Phil. 1:9–10). While some Christians have a special gift for discernment, every believer can use discernment for at least two purposes: (1) to understand God's calling and will in their life and the life of the church, and (2) to perceive and distinguish truth from falsehood. Discernment develops alongside the practice of all the previous spiritual disciplines. As a spiritual discipline, discernment depends entirely on the work of the Holy Spirit. Christians develop their ability to discern through prayer, Bible study and meditation, and fasting. As they become more sensitive to God's voice and promptings, their ability to discern God's plans and desires for their lives increases. Discernment benefits greatly from the joint search for God's will within the church. People are limited and imperfect beings who are also skilled in self-deception. Having the joint discernment of other Christians can keep an individual believer from this error.

> The fruit of solitude is increased sensitivity and compassion for others. There comes a new freedom to be with people. There is new attentiveness to their needs, new responsiveness to their hurts.
>
> RICHARD J. FOSTER, *CELEBRATION OF DISCIPLINE*

WHAT ARE BAPTISM AND THE LORD'S SUPPER?

THE Christian faith institutes *baptism* and *the Lord's Supper*, or *communion*, as part of congregational life, following Jesus Christ's teaching to do so. Depending on their beliefs, different churches use differing terms for these rites. *Sacrament* is usually the term of choice primarily in liturgical churches; it is understood to mean that the rite is in some way a means by which God extends his grace. *Ordinance* is often the term of choice primarily in nonliturgical churches, where it is understood to mean that the rite is a symbol of God's grace already present in the believer.

> There is one body and one Spirit—just as you were called to one hope when you were called—one Lord, one faith, one baptism; one God and Father of all, who is over all and through all and in all.
>
> EPHESIANS 4:4–6

Baptism

Baptism is one of the most important practices in the life of the church. The need for baptism is something that most Christians recognize. Jesus emphasized the importance of baptism when he commanded his disciples to "go and make disciples of all nations, baptizing them in the name of the Father and of the Son and of the Holy Spirit" (Matt. 28:19). Baptism is a reminder to Christians of Jesus Christ's death and resurrection and their unified relationship to God and other Christians through the Holy Spirit (Eph. 4:4-6). Committed Christians interpret baptism in different ways, but most Christians agree on the following points:

+ Baptism is central to the Christian faith and is not optional but a commandment.

+ Baptism is often a way for people to make their commitment to God public.

+ Baptism unifies Christians as members of the same body.

+ Baptism has no ultimate significance apart from faith in Jesus Christ.

What Happens During Baptism?

Although baptism ceremonies may look quite different among various churches, there are more similarities than differences.

1. Water is always present, whether it is in the form of a natural body of water, a baptismal font, a baptistery, a pool, or simply a bowl of water.

2. A church leader asks a few questions to give an opportunity for persons involved in the baptism to profess their faith outwardly, then asks for the support

of those present. In the case of infant baptism, those questions are for the parents and others present to make certain that the child will have Christian examples, support, and instruction to guide the child toward an eventual profession (public expression) of faith.

3. The leader sprinkles, pours, or immerses the person being baptized and says, "I baptize you in the name of the Father and of the Son and of the Holy Spirit."

How Did Baptism Originate?

People in the Old Testament did not baptize. However, some practices provide the background for the ideas and methods behind New Testament baptism. Purification rites and sacrifices in the Old Testament point to the need for cleansing of impurity, evil, and sin. In Christ, the functions of both water and blood came together.

✦ The blood of Christ cleans from all sin and evil (1 John 1:7).

✦ The blood of Christ atones for sins (Rom. 5:9).

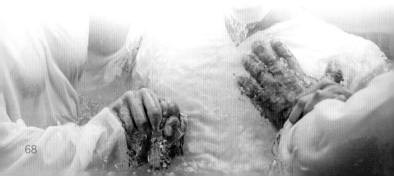

✦ Baptism symbolizes this cleansing in Christ's blood (1 Peter 3:21).

> The term *baptism* comes from a Greek word. The verb *baptizo* means "to cover in water, wash, dip, baptize."

A Symbol of Unity

The Bible teaches that baptism is an external symbol of Christian unity, signifying how a believer's faith and the work of the Holy Spirit unite Christians into one "body": the church. Jesus Christ's desire for his church is revealed in his prayer for all believers in John 17:23: "May they be brought to complete unity to let the world know that you sent me and have loved them even as you have loved me."

The Lord's Supper

The Lord's Supper, also called *Communion*, is a meal that Jesus had with his disciples the night before he was crucified. Jesus commanded them to remember his sacrifice by continuing to celebrate this supper. Years later, as an explanation of this sacrament, the apostle Paul wrote to Christians in Corinth,

I received from the Lord what I also passed on to you: The Lord Jesus, on the night he was betrayed, took bread, and when he had given thanks, he broke it and said, "This is my body, which is for you; do this in remembrance of me." In the same way, after supper he took the cup, saying, "This cup is the new covenant in my blood; do this, whenever you drink it, in remembrance of me." For whenever you eat this bread and drink this cup, you proclaim the Lord's death until he comes.

1 CORINTHIANS 11:23–26

The Lord's Supper is not a common meal. It is a time of fellowship, reflection, remembering, and spirituality. The Lord's Supper is related to how Christians understand who Jesus is and what he did in his earthly ministry.

Why Do Christians Celebrate the Lord's Supper?

✦ Jesus instituted the Lord's Supper and commanded his followers to observe it (Matt. 26:26–30; Mark 14:22–25; Luke 22:19–20; 1 Cor. 11:23–26). The Lord's Supper allows Christians to remember and celebrate with gratitude Jesus' birth, life and ministry, death, and resurrection.

✦ It is a way to proclaim the church's hope in Christ's return and forgiveness through the sacrifice of his body on the cross (represented by the "bread") and his shed blood (represented by the "cup" of wine or juice). Every time the Lord's Supper is celebrated, the gospel and Jesus' return are proclaimed (1 Cor. 11:26).

✦ It teaches new believers about who Jesus is and what he did for them (1 Cor. 11:24–26) and refreshes seasoned believers. Amid the pain of Israel's exile, the Old Testament records God's promise to make a new covenant with his people, writing his law on their hearts so their motivation to love and obey him would come from within (Jer. 31:32–34). The New Testament affirms that Jesus is the fulfillment of this new covenant, making possible the cleansing of a believer's conscience (Heb. 10:2, 22) and the renewing of their hearts through the Holy Spirit (1 Peter 1:23).

✦ It fosters unity with Christ and among believers. Unity is one of the central messages of the celebration and is symbolized in the one loaf of bread they all share (1 Cor. 10:17). In Christ, believers are one, like a loaf of bread. This agrees with Jesus' own prayer for the unity of the church (John 17:11; see also, 17:20–23). The New Testament makes it clear that Christian unity is not an option but part of God's plan for his people.

Other Names for the Lord's Supper

✦ Breaking of the Bread
✦ Holy Communion
✦ Table of the Lord
✦ The Eucharist

The Last Supper by Juan de Juanes, c.1562

What Does It Mean?

The Lord's Supper is meaningful to Christians in the following four areas:

✦ **Worship**. It is a way to worship Christ for his work, grace, love, and salvation. The Lord's Supper also anticipates the celebration of what Christians call *the wedding supper of the Lamb* (Rev. 19:9), a heavenly banquet at the end of the age, when Christ rules over all. The unity Christians can experience in the Lord's Supper as a special moment of celebration anticipates what life will be like with God in the new heavens and the new earth (Rev. 21:1–5).

✦ **Witness**. Participating in the Lord's Supper gives a testimony that Jesus died to forgive sins, was resurrected to give eternal life to those who come to him in faith, and will return as a victorious king (Matt. 26:29; 1 Cor. 11:26).

✦ **Edification**. Through the Lord's Supper, the Holy Spirit ministers to believers individually and as "Christ's body" on earth, a term used to refer to the church as a community (1 Cor. 10:16). It is a necessary time for reflection and introspection (1 Cor. 11:28), requiring believers to examine their lives, confess their sins, and ask God for forgiveness (1 Cor. 11:27–32). It is also a time for mutual instruction, forgiving past grievances, restoring broken relationships, and repenting of offenses against others (1 Cor. 11:28–29). It creates a strong bond of spiritual fellowship (1 Cor. 10:17).

> Participating in the Lord's Supper gives a testimony that Jesus died to forgive sins, was resurrected to give eternal life to those who come to him in faith, and will return as a victorious king.

✦ **Service**. The Lord's Supper is an occasion for Christians to serve each other, at the moment of the celebration itself as well as beyond.
Remembering the sacrificial gift of Christ on the cross (the gifts of the bread and the wine or juice) is a powerful motivation to extend this generosity to others (1 Tim. 5:8).

WHAT DO CHRISTIANS BELIEVE ABOUT DEATH AND HEAVEN?

For Christians, heaven is a source of hope, guidance, and meaning. It offers hope for a future destination, strength for life in the present, guidance for living as God's people today, and meaning and reassurance knowing there is more to life than this world.

Christians believe that when they die, they will go to a place of waiting in the presence of God (2 Cor. 5:8). Many theologians refer to this period between a Christian's death and Jesus Christ's return to earth as the *intermediate state*. The intermediate state is not a permanent place; rather, the whole creation waits for the final redemption at the end of time.

In popular culture, heaven evokes images of a cloudy, ghostlike existence, or angelic beings floating about among the clouds. It can also be portrayed as a place where people sing all the time, where all beings live as angels, and where everyone goes after death. The Bible teaches differently. And although it's not known exactly what or where this intermediate state is, it *is* where Jesus is present. However, the Bible teaches that the final destination of Christians is not an ethereal place but *the renewed heavens and earth* anticipated in Revelation 21.

The New Heavens and New Earth

When God renews all things, Christians will dwell together in the new heavens and the new earth (Rev. 21–22). According to the Bible, God created the universe for his glory and out of his desire for relationship. He intended all his creatures to relate to each other, to nature, and to himself in harmony. Humanity's main and great goal in life is to glorify God (Isa. 60:21; 1 Cor. 6:20, 31) and enjoy him forever (Phil. 4:4; Rev. 21:3–4). After human sin twisted God's original intentions, God, in his grace and faithfulness, planned to rescue his creation from the effects of sin through the saving work of Jesus on the cross (Rom. 8:18–27). As Christians find peace with God and each other, they can also begin this reconciliation with nature.

What Will the Renewed Heavens and Earth Be Like?

This process will have a glorious ending when Jesus Christ renews all things (Rev. 21:1). It will not be a different creation or a noncreation; it will be *this* creation renewed. God will restore his creation to its original glory and purpose. As if to close the circle, what God began at the garden of Eden (the book of Genesis) he will fulfill at

the end of the age (the book of Revelation). Not everything will be the same; some of the elements from the biblical idea of Eden will continue in the renewed creation, but others will end.

Christians understand that even if many things about the world to come are not clear, God still offers glimpses of heaven in this current world we live in—through the love people experience for and from others, in the majesty of nature's beauty and power, in the generosity and kindness of people in times of need, in the smile of a happy baby, in the loyalty and warmth of pets, in the tenderness and wisdom of old age, and in moments of deep emotional and spiritual connections with loved ones and himself.

Since emotions and relationships are a very important part of what it means to be human, Christians teach that there will be emotions and relationships in heaven, though they may not be exactly the same. They will be renewed emotions, emotions as they were meant to be from the beginning: joyful, satisfying, enriching, intimate, and refreshing. There will be no sorrow, or regrets, or guilt. Rather, love, compassion, gentleness, tenderness, and other emotions will find new heights and depths in heaven. There will be no brokenness, either emotional or physical. When Jesus returns, God will renew the bodies of those who have already died and those who are still alive when he comes.

WHAT WILL CONTINUE?

- ✦ Physical bodies
- ✦ Emotions (relationships)
- ✦ Nature
- ✦ Daily cycles
- ✦ Weather
- ✦ Animals, including pets
- ✦ Many activities, such as work, learning, science, art, and entertainment

WHAT WILL END?

- ✦ Evil
- ✦ The curse of sin and penalty of death
- ✦ Emotional and physical brokenness; suffering and sadness
- ✦ Human marriage; marriage recast in the relationship of Christ to his bride, the church

- ✦ War
- ✦ Famine
- ✦ The need for a temple to house God's earthly presence

ORIGINAL CREATION (GENESIS)	RENEWED CREATION (REVELATION)
Heaven and earth created, 1:1	Heavens and earth renewed, 21:1
Sun created, 1:16	No need of sun, 21:23
Night established, 1:5	No night there, 22:5
Seas created, 1:10	No more sea, 21:1
Death enters the world, 2:19	Death is no more, 21:4
Humanity is cast out of paradise, 3:24	Humanity is restored to paradise, 22:14
Sorrow and pain begin, 3:17	Sorrow, tears, and pain end, 21:4

What Are the Rapture and Tribulation?

The subjects of the Rapture and the Tribulation are often common topics in Christian circles and sometimes even mentioned in popular culture.

The phrase *The Rapture* comes from a New Testament passage that describes Christians, both alive and deceased, rising up to meet Jesus Christ in the air to live with him forever:

> *We who are still living when the Lord returns will not meet him ahead of those who have died. For the Lord himself will come down from heaven with a commanding shout, with the voice of the archangel, and with the trumpet call of God. First, the believers who have died will rise from their graves. Then, together with them, we who are still alive and remain on the earth will be caught up in the clouds to meet the Lord in the air. Then we will be with the Lord forever.*

1 THESSALONIANS 4:15-17 NLT

Although the Bible text clearly portrays the event, Christians have differing opinions about the timing and how it relates to the establishment of the new heavens and the new earth. Varying theories also exist about how it relates to the timing of an event called *The Tribulation*, a period preceding the new heavens and earth that is marked by trouble and persecution, as predicted by biblical prophets. Christians are united, however, in their belief that Jesus Christ will return to defeat evil, ruling and reigning as the supreme earthly King. In any scenario, they believe they will live with him in a place of safety, peace, and joy for eternity.

Jesus' Resurrection

Jesus' resurrection offers Christians an idea of what heaven may look like since the Bible teaches that (1) a Christian's future is tied to Jesus Christ's own resurrection (1 Cor. 15:12–34) and (2) Christ is the first example of all who will be raised into new life (15:20). Based on his experience, Christians expect:

The Doubting Thomas
by Carl Heinrich Bloch

+ **They will have a resurrected body that is a physical reality.** Future resurrected bodies will be like Jesus' own resurrected body (1 Cor. 15:42–49).

+ **They will recognize Christians they know.** Since Jesus' followers recognized him after his resurrection (Matt. 28:9, 17), they will recognize friends and loved ones who have resurrected bodies.

✦ **They will have physical bodies that are no longer subject to death.** Jesus' resurrected body was physical (Luke 24:39). He even ate with his disciples (Luke 24:41–43). Yet it was not a body like ours. Both Jesus' pre- and post-resurrection bodies were physical; the difference is about perishability. That is, natural bodies die; spiritual bodies do not. Sin has polluted and damaged natural bodies; they die and decay and are unfit for a future in God's presence. Just as God will renew this creation, also marred by sin, God will give believers renewed bodies that will not be polluted by sin, will not decay, and will be fit to live eternally in the presence of God.

What Happens When Non-Christians Die?

Just as Christians acknowledge the reality of heaven, they also recognize the reality of hell—that it exists as a place of punishment for those who choose to reject God's love—and that there is only one way to escape it: by surrendering to Jesus Christ and experiencing the renewal of their hearts (Matt. 10:28; 25:31–46; John 3:3; 1 John 5:12; Rev. 21:8).

Jesus replied, "I tell you the truth, unless you are born again, you cannot see the Kingdom of God."

JOHN 3:3 NLT

What Will Christians Do in Heaven?

The Bible does not give many details about activities in heaven, but Christians believe that because nature will be renewed to fulfill God's purposes, it is at least possible that much of the new creation will be similar to what we experience now. The best things about this world will just become better. Since work is also a form of worship and God meant for humans to help take care of his creation (Gen. 2:15), each person will develop and thrive with his or her own talents. They will no longer work in places that do not allow them to grow as individuals, or where they might be unappreciated, or where they cannot possibly be happy. God intended work to be a joyful activity—a way to fellowship with God by caring for his world. For this reason, Christians will have plenty of interesting things to do in the renewed creation. As with work, they imagine the same for learning, science, arts, and sports. The gifts and talents of painters, poets, athletes, and scientists will be used simply to worship God and provide for others' enjoyment.

> I saw "a new heaven and a new earth," for the first heaven and the first earth had passed away.
>
> REVELATION 21:1

QUICK REFERENCE: 14 KEY CHRISTIAN BELIEFS

WHAT are the key beliefs of the Christian faith? The core teachings of the Bible have defined Christianity for two thousand years. Virtually all Christians who seek to have a faith that is biblical hold to some form of these basic beliefs. Christians may not always agree on how they work out the details of their faith, but they mostly agree on certain essential truths:

1. God's Unity
2. God's Tri-unity
3. Human Depravity
4. Christ's Virgin Birth
5. Christ's Sinlessness
6. Christ's Deity
7. Christ's Humanity
8. The Necessity of God's Grace
9. The Necessity of Faith
10. Christ's Atoning Death
11. Christ's Bodily Resurrection
12. Christ's Bodily Ascension
13. Christ's Intercession
14. Christ's Second Coming

1. God's Unity

There is one—and only one—God, Creator of the universe (Ex. 20:2–3; Deut. 6:4; Isa. 43:10–11). He has always existed and will always exist.

2. God's Tri-unity

While there is only one God, he exists eternally in three Persons. In the Bible, the Father is called God (2 Thess. 1:2), the Son (Jesus) is called God (John 1:1–5; John 10:30-33; John 20:28; Heb. 1:8; Phil. 2:9–11), and the Holy Spirit is called God (Acts 5:3–4, 2 Cor. 3:17). He is one substance but three Persons in relationship (Matt. 3:16–17; 28:19; 2 Cor. 13:14). There are more than sixty passages in the Bible that mention the three Persons together.

3. Human Depravity

Since God is a personal Being, he wants personal relationships with human beings. Human depravity means that every human is spiritually separated from God, totally incapable of saving himself (Rom. 3:10–11). When Adam sinned, he died spiritually and his relationship with God was severed. Additionally, all of Adam's descendants are "dead in trespasses" (Eph. 2:1). Without a new birth (being created anew) no one can enter life (John 3:3).

4. Christ's Virgin Birth

Jesus was born as a result of a miracle (Matt. 1:18–23): Mary, Jesus' mother, became pregnant without ever having sexual relations. The doctrine of Jesus' Virgin Birth is not primarily about Mary's virginity and miraculous conception. Though this miracle fulfilled a preordained prophecy (Isa. 7:14), the reason it is essential has to do with God's supernatural intervention. Human sin is not merely something we do—it is who we are. It is inborn. Human depravity is transmitted from parents (Ps. 51:5; 1 Cor. 15:22; Rom. 5:12–15). Because God interrupted the natural birth process in the case of Jesus, Jesus did not inherit a sin nature. In other words, Jesus not only did not sin, he had no inclination to sin even when tempted. He was perfect.

5. Christ's Sinlessness

Christ was born of a virgin, and he did not suffer the effects of a sin nature. Throughout his life Jesus remained sinless (Heb. 4:15; 1 Peter 2:22). Because of sin, humanity could not have a relationship with God; but because Jesus did not sin, he was perfectly able to represent humanity (stand in their place) before God (2 Cor. 5:21).

6. Christ's Deity

The only way for humans to be restored spiritually to God was for God to build a bridge across the gap of separation. So God, while retaining his full God nature (John 1:1; Heb. 1:8), became a perfect man in Christ in order to bridge the chasm (Col. 2:9). If he is not both God and Man he cannot mediate between God and man (1 Tim. 2:5). Jesus Christ is the second Person in the Trinity.

7. Christ's Humanity

Jesus was also fully human. Jesus got tired; he slept; he sweated; he got hungry and thirsty (Heb. 2:14). Without being fully human, Jesus could not pay the price for human sin. He needed to be divine to have the power to *save* humanity, and he needed to be human in order to adequately *represent* humanity (John 1:14; Phil. 2:7). Christ had to be both divine and human.

8. The Necessity of God's Grace

Because of human depravity, humanity cannot save themselves (John 15:5; Rom. 9:16). It is by God's grace alone that salvation is possible (Eph. 2:8–9; Titus 3:5–7). God is right to call humankind to account for sin. However, by his grace, undeserving people will be united in fellowship with him and avoid judgment. Without God's grace, no one could come into relationship with God. Relationship with God is peace, joy, and eternal life itself (John 17:3).

9. The Necessity of Faith

Faith is trusting that God can and will save. No one can earn salvation (Heb. 11:6). No amount of good works can ever repay the debt that is owed to God. However, by trusting in him and thankfully accepting his gift of salvation, humanity can be united with God (Rom. 4:5). Faith is an individual act, but it is not a work. Faith is when a person trusts God to do what they could not do for themselves (Eph. 2: 8–9; Titus 3:5).

10. Christ's Atoning Death

The penalty for sin is death—not only physical death (separation of the soul from the body), but also spiritual death (separation of ourselves from God). The penalty owed to God was paid by Christ through his death on the cross. The acceptable payment had to be perfect, complete, and without fault. Christ, the perfect Man, gave himself in mankind's place (Mark 10:45; 1 Peter 2:24; 3:18), so that whoever believes in him will not die (physically and spiritually) but have everlasting life (John 3:16; 14:6).

11. Christ's Bodily Resurrection

The atoning death of Christ paid for sins (Rom. 4:25; 10:9), but the process was not complete until he had defeated death by being physically resurrected in the same body (Luke 24:3; John 2:19–21). Because Christ is the victor over death and the prototype of a new, glorified physical body, all of humanity will be resurrected and live forever in either heaven or hell.

A Christian Understanding of Evidence for the Resurrection

Jesus was a real person. At least thirty-nine ancient Jewish and Gentile sources apart from the Bible note his teachings, miracles, life, and death.

Many saw him dead, then alive. Some say Jesus merely fainted on the cross. Others say the people who saw him alive later were "hallucinating." But according to the Bible, Jesus' enemies and the Roman soldiers who executed him were satisfied that he was dead. After three days in the grave, five hundred people, as individuals and in groups, saw him over a period of forty days as he walked, ate, and preached (1 Cor. 15:3–8).

His followers changed radically. Jesus' disciples turned from "common people" into bold preachers, bravely facing persecution. Most died as martyrs for their faith (Acts 4:1–22; 12:1–3). It's reasonable to assume that people would not die for a religious belief if they knew that belief was a lie.

Why does it matter? Jesus' resurrection proved he was divine and that everything he taught and claimed is true.

12. Christ's Bodily Ascension

Christ died for mankind's sins and was physically resurrected for their salvation. Then forty days later, he was taken up ("ascended") bodily into heaven (Luke 24:50–51; Acts 1:9–10). Because Christ has ascended to the Father, the Holy Spirit now guides Christians, showing them where they are wrong and comforting them when they hurt (John 16:7). Jesus' going to the Father means their life is kept safe in heaven with God.

13. Christ's Intercession

Christ's bodily ascension allowed him to serve as mediator (or high priest) before God (Heb. 1:3; 4:15). In God's presence, Christ prays continually on his followers' behalf (Heb. 7:25; 1 John 2:1). Like a lawyer defends someone before a judge, so Jesus defends Christians before the bar of God's law and against the accusations of Satan (Rev. 12:10).

14. Christ's Second Coming

Just as Christ left the world physically, so he will return in the same manner (Matt. 24:30; Luke 12:40). For believers, his second coming is the hope of the world (Rev. 21:4; 22:12). When he returns, dead believers will receive their resurrected bodies (Col. 3:3–4). Believers that are alive when he returns will not die, but will be transformed into immortal, physical bodies (1 Cor. 13:12). Christ's bodily return to earth will be visible to all, and believers will rule with him in his kingdom and live with him forever (John 14:1–3). Those who do not believe will be separated from God's goodness forever (2 Thess. 1:7–9; Rev. 20:11–15).

How Christians View Salvation

In addition to these fourteen key points, two more essentials define how Christians view salvation:

1 *Inspiration of Scripture*

In order for Christians to have a sure foundation for what they believe, God revealed his Word (the Bible) as the basis of their beliefs. As Thomas Aquinas put it, "In order that salvation might the easier be brought to man and be more certain, it was necessary that men be instructed concerning divine matters through divine revelation," which is the Bible (*Summa Theologica* 1.1.1). Since Christians believe that God cannot err (Heb. 6:18), then neither can his Word (John 17:17). Without a divinely authoritative revelation from God, such as in the Scriptures, Christians could never be sure of the doctrines that are necessary for salvation.

2 *Method of Interpretation*

In addition, all the salvation doctrines are derived from the Bible by literal interpretation—that is, Scripture is true, just as the author meant it. By the historical-grammatical method of interpretation of Scripture (identifying the writer's original intended meaning by considering the text's grammar, genre, and historical and theological background), one can know *which* truths are essential for salvation.

THE APOSTLES' CREED

Jesus' Apostles did not write the Apostles' Creed. No one knows for certain when this creed was written, but references to and quotations of similar statements—known as the "Rule of Faith"—can be found in writings dating from as early as the second century AD. The title "Apostles' Creed" means that the creed contains the Apostolic tradition. The Apostles' Creed is the most universal of all Christian creeds. Many churches continue to recite and teach it.

Early creedal statements were very helpful for new Christians in understanding their faith, and new believers memorized and studied them before being baptized. It is quite possible that from these baptismal "formulas," the ancient church developed what we now call the Apostles' Creed:

I believe in God, the Father Almighty,

Maker of heaven and earth,

And in Jesus Christ, his only Son, our Lord;

*Who was conceived by the Holy Spirit
and born of the Virgin Mary;*

Suffered under Pontius Pilate;

Was crucified, died, and buried.

He descended into hell.

On the third day, he rose from the dead.

*He ascended into heaven and is seated
at the right hand of the Father;*

*From thence he will come to judge
the living and the dead.*

I believe in the Holy Spirit,

The holy catholic (universal) church,

The communion of saints,

The forgiveness of sins,

The resurrection of the body, and the life everlasting.

RESOURCES

Christian Apologetics, by Norman Geisler

Celebration of Discipline, by Richard J. Foster

Essential Truths of the Christian Faith, by R. C. Sproul

Evidence That Demands a Verdict and *More Than a Carpenter*, by Josh McDowell

Growing in Discipleship, by The Navigators

Is Believing in God Irrational? by Amy Orr-Ewing

Knowing God, by J. I. Packer

Mere Christianity, by C. S. Lewis

Reasonable Faith, by William Lane Craig

Rose Guide to Discipleship, by Rose Publishing

Spiritual Disciplines for the Christian Life, by Donald S. Whitney

The Case for Christ and *The Case for Faith*, by Lee Strobel

The Reason for God, by Timothy Keller

The Spirit of the Disciplines, by Dallas Willard

MADE EASY

by Rose Publishing

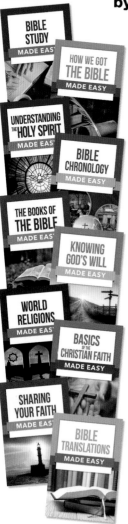

BIBLE STUDY MADE EASY
A step-by-step guide to studying God's Word

HOW WE GOT THE BIBLE MADE EASY
Key events in the history of the Bible

UNDERSTANDING THE HOLY SPIRIT MADE EASY
Who the Holy Spirit is and what he does

BIBLE CHRONOLOGY MADE EASY
Bible characters and events in the order they happened

THE BOOKS OF THE BIBLE MADE EASY
Quick summaries of all 66 books of the Bible

KNOWING GOD'S WILL MADE EASY
Answers to tough questions about God's will

WORLD RELIGIONS MADE EASY
30 religions and how they compare to Christianity

BASICS OF THE CHRISTIAN FAITH MADE EASY
Key Christian beliefs and practices

SHARING YOUR FAITH MADE EASY
How to share the gospel

BIBLE TRANSLATIONS MADE EASY
Compares 20 popular Bible versions

www.hendricksonrose.com